Spirit of Wilderness

An Inspirational Quotes Coloring Book for Nature Lovers

You belong among the wild flowers

THE
MOUNTAINS
ARE
CALLING
AND
I MUST
GO.
John Muir

THE WILDERNESS HOLDS ANSWERS TO QUESTIONS WE HAVE NOT YET LEARNED TO ASK

The CLEAREST WAY INTO THE UNIVERSE IS THROUGH A FOREST WILDERNESS.

John Muir

Look deep into nature and then you will understand everything better.

Albert Einstein

NATURE IS NOT A PLACE TO VISIT. IT IS HOME.

How lovely the silence of growing things

May you
touch fireflies
and stars,

dance with fairies
and talk to
the moon.

THE MOUNTAINS ARE MY BONES
THE RIVERS MY VEINS
THE FORESTS ARE MY THOUGHTS
AND THE STARS ARE MY DREAMS
THE OCEAN IS MY HEART
ITS POUNDING IS MY PULSE
THE SONGS OF THE EARTH WRITE
THE MUSIC OF MY SOUL

MOTHER NATURE
REVEALS HER SECRETS
TO THOSE WHO WALK
HER PATHS.
- SHIKOBA -

The earth does not belong to man. Man belongs to earth.

In Wilderness
lies
the Hope
of
the World.

John Muir

When setting out on a JOURNEY do not seek advice from those who have never left HOME.
-Rumi-

Nature
never
hurries
yet
everything
is
accomplished.

— Lao Tsu —

And into the Forest I go to loose my MIND and find my Soul

Coloring Books

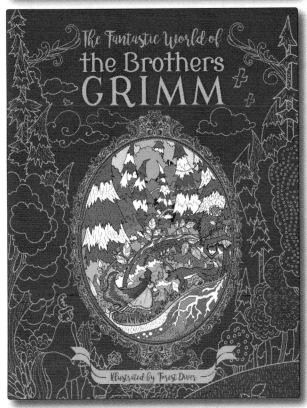

Coloring Book
ENCHANTING PRINCESSES, PONIES AND UNICORNS

ALICE'S ADVENTURES IN WONDERLAND
Illustrated by Forest Dawn

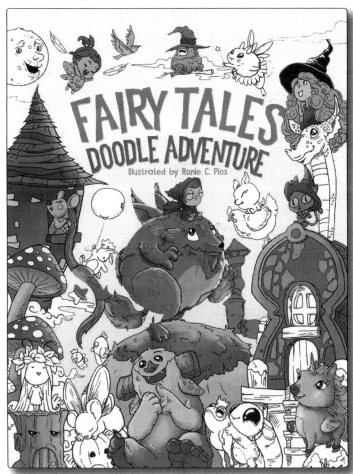

FAIRY TALES DOODLE ADVENTURE
Illustrated by Ronie C. Pios

Adult Coloring Book
Island Dreams
Return to Paradise

Illustrated by
Ika Sirana

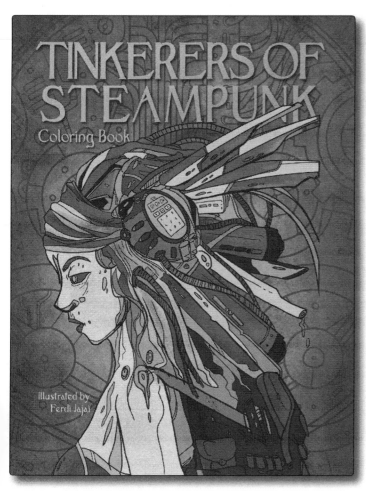

TINKERERS OF STEAMPUNK
Coloring Book

illustrated by
Ferdi Jajai

Storytroll Studios
The Hidden Spirits of the
Enchanted Forest
Coloring Book

Illustrated by Forest Diver

Coloring Book
Enchanting Mermaids

Finding Wonderland
Storytroll Coloring Book

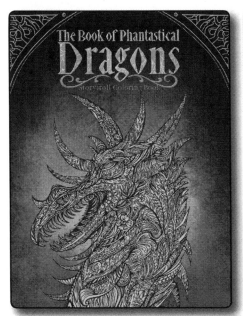

The Book of Phantastical **Dragons**
Storytroll Coloring Book

Storytroll Coloring Book
Impressions of Spring
Illustrated by MgA. Radana Planka

THE MANGA INVASION
COLORING BOOK
Illustrated by Boonchu

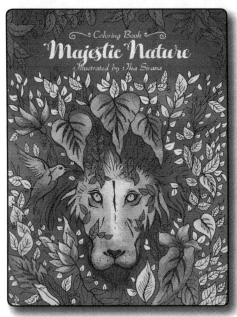

Coloring Book
Majestic Nature
Illustrated by Ika Sirana

Forgotten Creatures of the Hidden Forest
Storytroll Coloring Book
Illustrated by Ika Sirana

DINOMON
Invasion of the Dinosaur Doodles
Illustrated by Rosie C. Aw

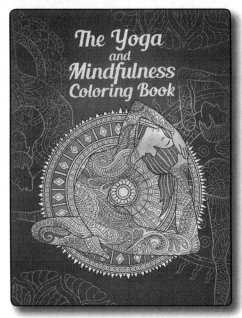

The Yoga and **Mindfulness** Coloring Book

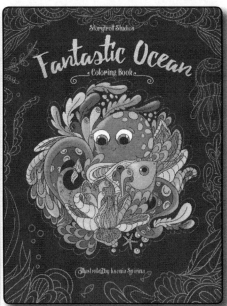

Storytroll Studios
Fantastic Ocean
Coloring Book
Illustrated by Ksenia Spirina

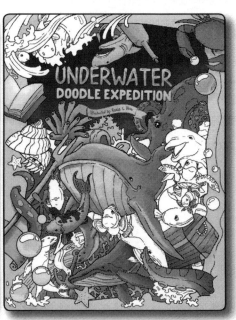

UNDERWATER
DOODLE EXPEDITION
Illustrated by Rosie C. Aw

Children's Books

Made in the USA
Middletown, DE
21 August 2018